BURNS UNIT

POETRY TO HEAL THE WOUNDS OF MEDICAL GASLIGHTING

JESS GREGORY

EDITED BY
KEVIN SAITTA

Cover & Interdesign by Written Tales.

Published by Written Tales.

This collection is dedicated to Dr. Marie — thank you for restoring (some of) my faith in the medical system and, more importantly, in my own self-advocacy skills.

SURVIVAL

This is a story of survival.

Not a story of triumph,
Success,
Or even resilience.

Not a story of lessons learned,
Of barriers broken,
Or examples set for others.

No dreams come true in this story.
No minds are changed,
No battles won.
No broken systems were overthrown.

This is a story of survival.

To all my fellow survivors, you are enough.

xx Jess

CONTENTS

FOREWORD

Burns Unit was conceived through my own experience of processing the trauma of long-term medical gaslighting and negligence. I was born with a genetic condition called Ehlers-Danlos Syndrome and live with several comorbid conditions. However, none of these were diagnosed until I was 27 years old, mainly due to our medical system's biased and broken nature.

Although this medical trauma has been slowly accumulating over the course of most of my life, *Burns Unit* follows my journey over the last four years, during which I became my sickest, and had a "sink or swim" moment - choosing to fight harder than ever for answers and relief. I feel like I suffered the most during this period, but also grew the most; for that, I am grateful.

This was also the time during which I discovered that I was far from alone in my traumatic experiences and that they were a symptom of a much larger epidemic of doctors gaslighting patients with rare and poorly understood diseases. While this has been heartbreaking, it has allowed me to let go of much of the guilt and shame that I previously felt, and for that, I am eternally indebted to my fellow chronic illness and disability warriors. This book is a love letter to our community and the almighty strength that we rally for each other in the darkest of times.

You'll notice the poems in this book take many different forms. I love combining old-style forms with modern subject matter (such as *Addiction* - a Petrarchan Sonnet about pill-shaming!), but as I've grown as a poet, I've developed more and more of an appreciation for modern writing styles, and their ethereal and sometimes even abstract nature. I have been particularly influenced by fellow disabled poet Maggie Bowyer — who has been an important mentor to me, and Eimear McBride — a wonderful novelist with a unique narrative voice.

Although *Burns Unit* is not a long book, it is a densely packed emotional journey in three stages, "Epiphany, Healing, and The Future," (much like my life over the past few years!) and as such, it is not something that was intended to be read in a day.

Kindly be aware that some of these poems might be triggering, especially if you've personally encountered medical trauma. My intention is for these poems to resonate with you, offering solace, a sense of connection, and a way to express your justified anger.

PART ONE
EPIPHANY

What if I wasn't the problem?

What if there was no level of preparation, patience, or
finesse that could have changed my fate? What if the
only ones who could have saved me had no interest in
doing so?

Then what could I possibly do but crumble, into a thou-
sand tiny, glass shards —
reflecting someone who wasn't in control of their own
destiny?

What if the rigid, well-behaved woman I had crafted never held me together, but down, just like those who profited from her?

What if everyone else who denied it could simply never admit that the same thing could happen to them?

What then?

1
POOL PARTY

Chasing after her as the party rages on. / "Please
    stop!" / Tears rolling down my face. /
Hearing the familiar splashing sound - she's
    launching herself into the water / blissfully
unaware of the danger that awaits. / Other guests
    equally unphased / They're here / why
shouldn't she be?

Am I the only one who sees that she's drowning?

Diving in as she slips below the surface / sea of frol-
    icking legs obscuring my vision / Where is she? /
    Where is she!?

Too late / Cold and lifeless on the pool floor. / Drag-
    ging her dead weight / limp / damp
/ empty home for what she once was.

Waking up drenched / this time in sweat / but also in
    clarity / She was never going to wait. /
The party was now / and she wouldn't be caught dead
    with a life left unlived. / She was taught to believe
    she could / so she died doing it.

2

THE LETTER I WISH I COULD SEND

Dear Jess,

I see you standing there / Flight or freeze / But no more fight.

Constantly uncomfortable / And wondering / "Is it *really* that bad? Or does everyone feel this way?"

Yes / It really *is* that bad.

In fact, one day / You'll look back / And realise / Your entire personality has warped / Into something / You barely recognise. / Angry and selfish / Yet somehow / Complacent and submissive. / Hard-working / But cutting life's corners / All without hope / Of anything / In particular to follow.

Caved in and simply waiting to emerge / As the person / Everyone else *thinks* you should become. / I wish I could tell you that things will get easier…

But instead / *You* will get stronger / Smarter / More discerning / More righteous / Less afraid.

Your shame will turn to rage / Your rage will turn to action / Your action will turn to change / Your change will turn to progress. / You'll go from screaming: "Everything feels hard *all* the time, and I don't know why!" / To declare: "Everything feels hard, but *nothing* will stop me from finding out why!"

You'll howl at the moon / Thinking of your misfortunes / And of the ones who propagated it.

You'll pine for those who never left your side / And for the years you've collectively lost.

You'll despair / Deeper than you ever thought possible.

You'll find relief / Sweeter than you ever imagined.

You'll realize the terrible pain / And power / In knowing that all you really have is yourself / But in the end / That's all you'll need.

3
VISIBLE ILLNESS
DEPICTIONS OF PAIN AND INJURY.

Look at these eyes, so sunken in,
Dark under sides, vein-laced skin.
Completion is pale, my spirit is stale,
What is it that you don't see?

Pupils dilated, I'm getting frustrated,
Just can't seem to get through my day.
Each wobbly step is lacking in pep,
I *know* that you've seen me this way —

Sat on the floor, massaging my jaw,
Telling you, "No! I can't talk anymore!"
Not five more minutes, I'm reaching my limit,
Can you not see that I'm sore?

Hives, rashes, bruises, bashes,
Hair falling off of my head and my lashes,
Try not to speak of my flares and my crashes,
Haven't you *seen* all my blisters and thrashes?

Hear all these joints, cracking and popping?
See trigger points, pulsing and throbbing?
See all these pills, that I keep on popping!?
Don't pretend that you don't see.

Eating so bland, with fragrances banned,
Reaching for coffee with trembling hands,
Surely you *know* why I canceled those plans!
How is it that you don't see?

What is it that it would take to persuade,
Break down the walls of this cruel masquerade,
To shatter the glass of your comfortable view,
That everyone here lives a life just like you?

What is it that you don't see?
How is it that you don't see?
Why is it that you won't see...

...The visible illness in me? [1]

—————————————

1. Visible Illness originally appeared in issue 2 of *Wishbone Words*.

4

ARE YOU GETTING ENOUGH SLEEP?

How long does it take you to get to sleep each night?

Are you waking up frequently? / Are you getting *enough* sleep? / If not, that could be a big contributor to your fatigue.

It's important not to lie in bed for too long though / That could make your pain and stiffness much, much worse. / The best way to fix that is to exercise more.

Oh? You're in pain because you're injured again? / That will be because you over-exercised! / It's important to take care of yourself, / Especially while you have all this extra time; / Don't spend your energy on too many unnecessary things. / Withdrawing from your regular activities isn't healthy, of course.

Keep in touch with all your friends / We need them to
keep an eye on your mental health / Especially
now that you're on those antidepressants. / They
should help you a lot. / Well, after the first five
weeks of complete physical and mental instability
have passed....

And if you take them at the same time every day, with
enough food, enough water, / And without any
conflicting medications... / And, if they happen to
suit your personal brain chemistry.

Definitely don't stop taking them.

Unless, of course, / They stop you from getting
enough sleep.

5
SPRING CLEANING
BLOOD & ABUSE.

Growth. Change.
Fresh sheets, light doonas.
Soft, pastel colours,
And ducklings,
Taking their first swim.

Flowers blooming,
Blasting,
Their toxic spores
Up my nose.

Chased out
By hot, salty water,
With a side of visceral,
Green gunk.

Sunshine piercing,
Burning,
Threatening,
To mutate precious cells
Into something,
Unspeakable.

Blood-soaked cloths,
From oozing sores
On hands and ankles,
As I crawl,
Dripping, aching,

Scrubbing and scrubbing,
And scrubbing,
This ancient wood —
No longer alive
But still able to bear
The marks
Of your abuse.

6

THREE TANKAS ON TRAUMA
DEPICTIONS OF PTSD SYMPTOMS

I

8 long years have passed,
Yet you make my blood run cold.
Body can't forget,

Thief who robbed me of my youth
And stained my once bright future.

II

Sweaty, sleepless nights
Follow cold and lifeless days.
Invisible walls,

Crafted from your echoed voice
And lack of recognition.

III

Words can't heal these wounds
But they sure can make them worse.
Every raging voice,

Reminds me of your cruelty
And my wasted potential.

7
YOU'VE BEEN LIED TO

They say that belief comes from seeing,
But the two are not so intertwined.
Denial and hate are not uncommon,
I guess it *does* cost to be kind.

Stones are cast even by sinners,
Seems that was their plan from the start.
Their sticks left your bones still intact,
But the words sure did tear up your heart.

The world let you think things were different,
That they would respond to your tears.
To you, they were all but *in*different,
And left you in limbo for years.

What's worse is they seemed unremorseful,
For shaving years off of your life.
How could they lack all recognition,
For the role that they played in your strife?

You'd think after taking an oath,
They'd respect the great power they wield,
But instead, they rejected all growth,
And held it up more like a shield.

The question that truly is frightening,
Is where do you turn to from here?
Your trust and your spirit lay broken,
And no one will lend you their ear.

8

NORMAL

You told me this was normal;
Comparing it
With your own experience.

Many examples made
Of your success;
A roadmap
To being more like you.

Moulding my ego
With your decree,
That this was not just possible,
But preferable.

Gently laying blame,
With sullied memories
And preconceived notions
Of what it was,
To be someone,
Less, like you.

False prophets
And lofty expectations —
A slow-acting poison,
Tricking me
Out of my youth, will,
And identity.

Stripped bare,
To a survivalist's instincts
And a chameleon's scales.

Broken,
And unable to be re-built
In your image.

9
SOMATIC, NOT PSYCHO
DEPICTIONS OF MIGRAINES, SEIZURES, MEDICAL GASLIGHTING.

Freezing seascape in my brain,
Taunted by the dust and rain,
Piercing through the silent morn',
Peaceless, even in my dorm.

Pressure mounting 'neath my eyes,
Dreading clear and bright blue skies.
No more strolling in the park;
Serotonin breaks my heart.

Popping, crackling when I hear
Soundbites striking like a spear.
Violent waves around me crash,
When'er I see a gleam or flash.

The wind, it swirls like beating wings,
The blurry world around me spins.
Yet you insist I workout more,
As I'm convulsing on the floor.

Threats perceived from my direction
Kill my chance at your protection.
Shameless, in your use of stealth
To weaponize my mental health.

It's clear you have no will to learn,
So let's just part on awkward terms,
Strident in my quest for more,
I walk four-legged to the door —

And turn my head to softly mutter,
"Somatic but not psycho, f*cker."

10

NEVER ENOUGH

Chased —
By a wide-eyed girl in love.

Clung to —
Like a fading summer romance.

Music felt like glitter
On my fingertips —
Tickled,
But never held firm.

In its beauty,
Another plane reflected,
Transcending,
Chains of my self-loathing.

It's wholeness,
And the holes in my heart,
Were surely a puzzle
To be solved.

But I was wrong.

While transformative,
Its power, too ethereal,
Would never speak
On my behalf.

Instead, summoning demons,
But never an exorcist.
Unstitching wounds,
But never cleaning them.

Grief and rage
Blistering and burning,
Conveying so much,
But never making me understood.

And so, I learned:

Hope without reason
Is folly.

Grief without mourning
Is suffering.

Fear without courage
Is cowardice.

Anger without resolve
Is destruction.

Beauty without purpose
Is why music alone —
Was never enough. [1]

----

1. Never Enough originally appeared in the *Music* issue of *The Sour Collective.*

11

ADDICTION
MEDICAL GASLIGHTING & SUBSTANCE ABUSE.

So, you want to talk about addiction?
With assumptions so coloured and many.
Do you want to call out my conviction?
'Cause my pills still consume each last penny.

Your cold shoulder once gave my heart friction,
On the long road to get just a slither,
Of the treatments that ended restriction,
For a girl who was starting to wither.

Now to think of you I just feel saddened,
'Cause how could it not leave a man maddened?
To know that his colleague would deny care,
Seated across from him in that same chair.
See that his trappings of ego and wealth,
Shield him no longer from fickle, ill health.

12

MANDRAKE

I was born a tiny, shrieking sapling,
Lacking roots but sprouting branches.
Being ripped from my natural state
To restore yours.

Handle with gloves:
Bark may lead to bites,
From insects making their home
In white, bleeding sores,
If they don't drown first
In their sticky residue.

Funny smells
Attract dabbling fingers,
Commodifying mystical properties
I'd never need,
If people just left well enough alone.

Put on your ear muffs
So you can harvest me,
Before my scream reaches full force.
Cut off my head
So you can count my rings
And declare me the wisest of all your victims.

13

I KNOW WHY THE CAGED BIRD WRITES

To capture her world behind bars / even if people
    think she's from Mars. / To pour out the
dreams in her heart / when she knows they no longer
    can pass.

Her cage strung so high / and her vocal cords fried /
    from screaming / for help that won't come. / Her
    wings are too heavy to fly / so she can't simply
    make for the sky.

Instead, she transforms her despair / when she feels
    that she's going nowhere. / For none of
us truly can heal / until we believe the pain's real.
Shame she's dependent on rhyme / to take the sting
    out of this / ~~crime~~ injustice

PART TWO
HEALING

The most difficult lesson we'll ever have to learn?
That evolution's spark doesn't always discern.
Was the light-peppered moth so inferior to the dark
When it wouldn't hide away in our human-stained bark?
A response to pressure, a way to survive
Rarely reflects what our soul needs to thrive.

14
THE FALL

You took me for a sinner,
And it took me too long
To realize,
I'd been cast out
And left to bleed.

But by each slither
Of the mouse,
I discovered,
I could actually *become* a sinner,
Who made their own way to the orchard —

Stuffing their rucksack
With more fruit,
Than they could ever need,
All the while calling
Fellow angels to do the same.

An invitation for you,
Not just to despise us,
But fear us,
As we sit fat and happy —

Spitting out your useless seeds,
And suckling
At the apple's teat,
Rather than your fragile ego.

Somehow surprised,
That clipping our wings
Landed us on the ground.
Soft flesh bruised,
But ready to sprout anew
In fertile soil.

15
BLACK DOG BOOGIE
BLOOD, VIOLENCE & DEPRESSION

Footsteps in the distance, inhuman and unkind.
My hands begin to clench, and my teeth begin to
    grind.
Pant! Pant! Pant! I can hear his stinking breath,
And know that I will feel it 'fore I see his silhouette.

With eyes as dark as night, and deeper than the sea.
He's licking his black chops before he sets his sights
    on me.
He lunges at my chest, it makes my body start.
I've heard his growling many times — its motion
    shakes my heart.

Saliva dripping down, and sticking to my skin,
Claws and teeth are drawing blood as they sink
    deeper in.
No one knows I'm here, it's that on which he preys.
He makes you think you can't escape from his
    demonic gaze.

There's buzzing in my ears, and fog before my eyes.
I know I could roll over — just accept that I'm his
    prize.
His weight is pressing down on me, my heart begins
    to race.
He thinks that he's the hunter, but I'll put him in his
    place!

We've done this dance before; I know the steps he'll
    make
Though it surely won't be easy with my sanity at
    stake!
My limbs are so damn heavy as I push against his
    might;
I look him squarely in the face, inviting him to fight.

He's clinging to my neck, as I shuffle t'ward the door.
The first step is the hardest, though, there are always
    many more.
The only move he has is to get inside my head.
Desperately he howls at me: "Just go back to bed!"

Alas, he finds his clumsy paws no longer match my
    stride.
I'm opening the door, as he whimpers by my side.
Now I see the golden path that waits outside this
    room;
If I expose his evil ways, he'll vanish in a plume!

As I step into the light, his tiny eyes slam shut.
Once a fearsome wolf, now a frightened little mut.
No doubt he'll try to stalk me for a little time, yet,
But every step I choose to take diminishes his threat. [1]

Dedicated to David Hulbert

---

1.   Black Dog Boogie originally appeared in issue 5 of *Wishbone Words*.

16

EMPTY

DEPRESSION & BURNOUT

Sometimes,
The most painful sensation
Is emptiness.

No guilt, grief, or rage
Can compare,
To the space
They leave in their wake.

Their boundless capacity
Inflates you,
Like a helium balloon.

But when you finally
Poke
Enough holes in their story,
They leave you —

Thin-skinned
And over-stretched,
From endless exertion
At your own expense.

17
GHOST STORY

Ghosts and ghouls have many tales,
And people search to no avail:
Castles, crypts, and haunted jails,
Seeking sleek and slimy trails.

Yet others *fear* to see their veil,
And rather hide their face and wail.
An otherness they must curtail,
Lest it, their fragile minds derail.

But *ghastliest* of ghostly grails,
Is he whom in yourself prevails,
Re-visit not abandoned trails,
Lest thy true nature be unveiled.

The angry phantom makes you pale,
Morals crumble, judgement fails.
Stings the skin like frozen hail,
An empty void and windless sails.

No burning sage can calm this gale,
A bitter battle, tooth and nail,
Just wretched pain and deep inhale,
Until your specter's spirit's stale.

18
FREEDOM

Walking's never something that I thought that I
 would lack,
I'm sick of spending so much time just flat upon my
 back.

Freedom comes in many forms, we can't always
 choose our own.
These limbs are unreliable, so I'll be rolling home.

Freedom comes in many forms, and sometimes it's a
 choice,
Today I chose to hop on board the self-propelled
 Rolls-Royce.

Some people say I've given up, that it's a last resort,
And so to all those skeptics, I offer this retort:

I no longer dream of studios, nor I of concert halls,
No longer dream of four white men behind a thin
 white wall.

Now I just crave freedom, in all its many forms,
All I want is to find a way to dance through this long
storm.

The freedom to say "yes!" when someone calls with
plans,
The freedom to see Belgium and its surrounding
lands.

The freedom to be home alone without fear and
dread,
The freedom on a "bad" day, to still leave my bed.

The freedom to leap up and write when inspiration
strikes,
The freedom to find brand new things I do and do not
like.

For this, I must leave the cozy house in which I live,
Many things still make this hard, which I try to
forgive.

I cannot change my body, I cannot change my life,
But I can grant myself this tool to save myself some
strife.

I don't need your permission; you cannot make
me beg.
That's a freedom I'll still have, even without these
legs.

I don't care if you disapprove, I don't care if you're
    friendly.
You won't stop me falling down, from being so damn
    bendy!

I hope that you'll accept me, but even if you don't,
I've finally learned to back myself and don't need you
    to dote.

I think that's true freedom, to know and love yourself,
Even if you'll always wish that you had better health.

19

JULY 15, 2022
MEDICAL TRAUMA, DERMATILLOMANIA.

The first thing I saw
was the crusty outline
of a long-forgotten pain patch
peeking from the sleeve of a satin blouse.

Luminous skin tint
not quite concealing
pale, sallow undertones
unfit for a sun-kissed face.

Glassy, dilated pupils
of a struggling liver
hidden behind thick, golden frames.
While the gentle
not quite
pleasant aroma
of pampers
hinted that a shower was long overdue.

Her flaking hands *unfolded*
revealing chalky regrowth
behind sunset, gel nails
cuticles picked raw.
As she reached
for a large
grey tablet
years
and years
and years
of observations
and more importantly
sources just in case
I turned out to be like the others.
Uncrossing her legs
she looked me in the eye.

Masked and ready
to conduct business so routine
it no longer provoked fear
or hope, just a vague sense of duty to share
a CV of pain and neglect
and to pay for the privilege.

20

THREE TANKAS ON HEALING
WOUNDS & SCARS

I

Even shallow wounds
Were once deep as the ocean;
Stung by salt water.

Closing slowly like a clam,
Protecting pearl-white treasure.

II

The thickest of scars
Still fade from purple to grey.
Natural wonder.

Should we not rejoice in the
Endless nature of healing?

III

Love and listening,
Are the *only* things that heal
From the inside out.

Stitch up your wounds with the words
Exchanged with kindred spirits.

21

THREE TANKAS ON CHRISTMAS

I

Confronting the things
Our body now denies us,
Feels like punishment,

For another person's crime;
Especially at Christmas.

II

People I don't know,
Argue 'round a table, full
Of food I can't eat.

It's the most wonderful time,
To establish boundaries.

III

Cruel nostalgia,
Why would you let me believe
An imagined past —

Where fruit mince pies were enough,
To fulfill a painless life? [1]

------

1. Three Tankas on Christmas originally appeared in *Written Tales* vol 3: *Tis the Season* under the title: *A Chronically Ill Christmas.*

22

SCABS

Scabs are gross.
Half-formed coverings
For recent traumas.
Lingering,
Until the body decides
It's time to grow thicker skin.

Giving way,
To a bloody mess
Under the slightest pressure.
Only to return –
Pussier, crustier,
And more liable to fail than before.

23
THE GREAT WAVE
SUICIDAL IDEATION

I stand atop the rocks,
Too far from the shore, but too high from the sea,
Fantasising,
About the great wave
That could hit me at any moment.

What would it be like to see death coming
And know there was nothing you could do?

Would it be a moment of pure, unadulterated fear?
Or of awe, in the face of nature's raw and unforgiving
    power?
The final push I need to accomplish something
    extraordinary?
Or the final blow in accepting my powerlessness?

Rocky terrain softens,
To a bed of flowers
And I lay my spinning head on it's colourful tapestry.

A roar fills my ears and I'm engulfed in blue.
Pain and power course through my body like never
    before
As their embrace immobilises me
In the great unknown.

24
DENNIS

"I WAS BORN at a very young age," he began, chuckling away at his own paternal joke. Spinning yet another tall tale to mixed responses was a large imposing man with a soft heart under those layers of militant discipline.

Is that why he saw through my facade so easily? -

The good girl with the wild heart and the burning ambition. The sweet girl with the vengeful soul and a suitcase full of grief.

Beneath the one-liners, sausage rolls, and sharp-edged jabs, two wounded souls recognised each other.

The day after I handed in my resignation, he bounded up to me with a wicked grin, "was it something I said?" He prodded.

I knew what he really meant - "I'll miss you."

"Kind, but non-nonsense," he wrote on my reference,

I think it's the greatest compliment I've ever received.

PART THREE
THE FUTURE

If you upset me,
Trust I won't run, scream or hide.
Instead, you may find

Unflattering poetry,
Posted about you online.

25
CUT OUT MY TONGUE
DEPICTIONS OF PAIN AND TORTURE

Cut out my tongue like you don't have a choice.
Crumple my lungs and tear out my voice.
Dismember my fingers and unplug my phone,
Shut off my computer and send me back home.

Continue to treat me with fear and disgust,
I'll keep on exposing your wounds of mistrust.
Cut into my soul with a knife lined by rust.
Though infected, my spirit won't wither to dust.

I'll keep my mouth open and let them all see,
Hands reaching out to all those who need me.
My lungs will still carry the force of my rage,
My voice will still find its way onto a page.

Cut out my tongue, and I'll barely scowl,
But at the right moment, I'll let out a howl,
Don't care if you think that my protest is foul,
You've no way to stop me from causing a row.

Think I'd roll over and wave the white dove?
Accept the corruption and kiss your pale glove?
You may take my money, my faith, and my youth,
But never my power in speaking the truth.

26

NEW YEAR'S EVE

Remnant vibrations
Of another's celebration,
Snake their way into my bed.

They light up my brain,
With pleasure and pain,
Of parties and rites, one forgets.

Some just surpassed me
And more did outlast me,
But some hit me square in the chest.

Though wavelengths were fickle,
My CNS rippled —
Puppeteering me to move
Nonetheless.

Adrenaline rising,
My symptoms disguising,
Clouding, this bridge of unrest.

The hope and the fear
Which through me did sear,
The knowledge,
That things were not fixed.

Though seemingly wise,
Each coin has two sides,
And flips when you're put to the test.

27
THERE ONCE WAS A GIRL IN A CHAIR

I

There once was a girl in a chair,
At which folks 'round town loved to stare.
Was it such a surprise
That she had useless thighs?
She just couldn't see why they cared.

II

There once was a girl from down under,
Whose wheelchair was louder than thunder,
Folks were never surprised
When she did arrive —
She found it a bit of a blunder!

III

There once was a girl in a chair,
Who harbored a growing despair.
All questions directed
To her sweet intended.
Had she just vanished into thin air?

IV

There once was a girl with a cane,
Despite this fact, she was still vain.
Folks sure got a shock
When they saw her bright frock,
But why should her fashion sense wane?

V

If there once was a girl in a chair,
Of which people seemed unaware,
And they only could speak
To more able physiques,
Then...was she actually there?

VI

There once was a girl in the know,
Who ran out of f*cks long ago.
If you ruin her day
With your ableist ways,
She might just roll over your toes.

Dedicated to Kit Millais

28

THE CRUELTY OF THE NIGHT
AFTER THE IMMORTAL WORDS OF DYLAN THOMAS

Do not go gentle into that first light,
Youth should burn and rave until the sight
Of sunrise, on a bold new day.

For those whose wounds of history flay,
Cry tears that do not blur their sight,
They rage, rage, against the cruelty of the night.

They know that these glass-case displays,
Mark not alone a proud new day,
Cannot go gentle into that first light.

While differences still spark a fight,
They feel each small and slimy slight,
They rage, rage, against the cruelty of the night.

Too thankful for ancestral might
To just succumb to Groundhog Day?
Do not go gentle into that first light.

My friends, until your lungs give way,
Reject their story of our plight!
Do not go gentle into that first light
But rage, rage, against the cruelty of the night.

29
THE LILY
GRIEF & DEATH

Some say that the Lily is a flower
Of grief; a gift, that sheaths our guilt and shame.
Performative empathy, emerging
From a wreath that's soon tossed and forgotten.

Yet to me, the Lily is a flower
Of peace. No milestone of death, but of
Ever-changing currents of life, of
Seasons. For whom death is both cyclical
And expected. No pure, white, unsullied peace,
But peace in the imperfect,
Gritty, ruthless, and unjust nature of living.

Dedicated to Maggie Bowyer

30
COCKROACH
VIOLENCE & SYSTEMIC OPPRESSION

Screamed at and spat on,
You're no threat to us.
Stepped on and beaten,
We'll never be crushed.

Each droplet of poison
Is never too much.
We'll keep on surviving
Down here in the dust.

Slandered and smeared,
But you'll still hear us chirp,
As we scuttle around corners
And claw through the dirt.

Determined, you hunt us
Till the ends of the earth.
All you see are germs,
But we know our worth.

Though burnt by your ire,
Our luck won't dry up.
We're too smart to drown
in your sweet wine-filled cup.

Starve us or choke us,
We won't be bereft.
You could cut off our heads
And we'd *still* have time left.

For this persecution,
Though endlessly cruel,
Will never destroy us,
Your wasteland, our fuel.

Dedicated to Niousha Afal

ABOUT THE AUTHOR

Jess (she/her) is an Australian/Anglo-Indian woman who has been living in Belgium since 2019. Shortly after this re-location, she had a significant health crisis which forced her to not only confront her current health problems but also the trauma she sustained from navigating the problematic medical system as an undiagnosed youth.

Over the course of the next two years, she would be diagnosed with the genetic connective tissue disorder — Hyper-mobile Ehlers Danlos Syndrome, and several of its associated co-morbidities, including Fibromyalgia, Migraine with Aura, Mast Cell Activation Disorder, and Postural Orthostatic Tachycardia Syndrome. Prior to this, she had already been living with diagnoses of Asthma, Post-Viral Fatigue Syndrome, Essential Tremor, Menorrhagia, and Premenstrual Dysphoric Disorder, but she knew something still wasn't adding up.

The overwhelming nature of having so many diagnoses (many of which are poorly understood and difficult to treat!) eventually prompted Jess to make the difficult decision to leave her first career as a classical musician (a trombone player) and focus on her well-being. She is still disabled by her conditions and cannot do many of the things she would like. However, she is more at peace after accepting her disabled body for what it is and rejecting the able-bodied standards that she once thought she had to adhere to.

Jess has found fulfillment in using her experiences to advocate for other members of the chronic illness and disability community. Above all, she seeks to encourage society to broaden their understanding of what a disabled person "should" look like, championing greater and more diverse representation of invisible and dynamic disabilities.

Jess is also eager to raise awareness of the flaws in the Western, modern medical model, and how patients with chronic conditions often fall through the cracks. She works with medical professionals and allies to help them understand how to best support people who have rare conditions or who are still undiagnosed.

Despite writing always being an important part of her advocacy, Jess only re-connected with poetry in the past few years, something which has been deeply cathartic for her. In combination with "a f*ck ton of therapy," it has helped her to process the immense trauma of growing up in chronic pain and feeling the need to pretend to be someone she was not.

Jess' poetry has appeared in "Wishbone Words," "The Sour Collective," and "Written Tales." She also writes educational and creative non-fiction pieces, which have been published by "Love What Matters," "The Mighty," and "Missive Mag," as well as on her own website www.delicatelittlepetal.com.

When not writing, Jess loves reading, swimming, vintage fashion and makeup, terrible reality TV, and spending time with her husband, Haydn, and their cat, Adora.

ACKNOWLEDGMENTS

Thank you to Written Tales for making my dream come true and publishing a collection of poetry about the modern epidemic of medical gaslighting! I appreciate the space you have created to tackle sensitive and challenging subjects, and uplift diverse voices.

I'd also like to thank the rare and precious healthcare providers throughout Belgium who have helped me restore enough of my health and sanity to make this collection a reality.

I would not be here without the love and support of my friends Kit, Stacey, Caitlyn and David, who have consistently stuck by my side throughout the most painful and unpredictable moments of my life, despite their own challenges. Nor without the influence of my parents, Robyn and Luke, who have always supported my creative endeavours, and taught me the value of self-awareness and emotional intelligence. Thank you for always seeing (and loving) me for me, despite the changing scenery...and for texting me in the middle of the night when you see spelling errors in my work.

I also owe a huge debt of gratitude to the online chronic illness and disability community, who have provided me with support, advice, and relatability that I could never have found anywhere else, and for helping me to become a better ally to all members of our community. You are as important to me as any of my "face-to-face" friends, and I dream of the day when my health is stable enough for me to travel and meet some of you!

I'd like to thank Maggie Bowyer, one of my most important poetry role models, not only for helping to re-spark my initial love of poetry, but also for providing invaluable feedback and encouragement during the development of this collection.

I'd also like to thank my fellow teammates at Wishbone Words for introducing me to the thriving online writing community, and for carving out a much-needed space for disabled and neuro-divergent voices.

Finally, thank you to my best friend, husband, and life partner, Haydn. You have stood by me as I faced my worst fears, and have explored and adapted to a whole new way of life by my side. Thank you for encouraging me to rest, but still getting angry on my behalf when I run out of energy, I love you.